NEW ZEALAND
KIWIFRUIT
COOK BOOK

JAN BILTON

IRVINE HOLT

CONTENTS

All recipes in this book use standard level measurements.

FOREWORD

Kiwifruit, 'Actinidia Chinesis', is native to the Yangtse Valley in China where it is called 'Yang Tao'.

Eighty years ago, kiwifruit vines were introduced to New Zealand where they flourished in the rich soils and temperate climate. New Zealanders called the vines, Chinese Gooseberries, for the original fruit was small, prickly, with a distinctive but unrefined taste.

It took more than 40 years to develop the fruit of today. Experimenting and breeding by N.Z. Horticulturalists increased the size, refined the flavour, improved the keeping qualities. The fruit came into wider use on N.Z. tables.

The unique, fresh taste soon found acceptance with connoiseurs in other lands — large scale exports commenced, to aid marketing the name was changed, and the kiwifruit became established as an exotic fruit internationally.

New Zealand is a South Pacific nation, where, because of the gentle climate and clean air, foods grow in abundance. Animals graze outdoors all year, the surrounding ocean is rich in seafood, tall mountains contain wild game, the rivers are world famous for their trout. It is no wonder that cooking is a N.Z. pastime.

This N.Z. Kiwifruit Cookbook brings together some of the country's favourite kiwifruit recipes and introduces some exciting new ideas for using this versatile fruit.

Publisher: Irvine Holt, P.O. Box 28019, Auckland 5, New Zealand.
Photography: Rees Osborne, Illustrations: Robert Bilton
Printed In New Zealand by Cox and Dawes Ltd.
© Copyright 1986 Irvine Holt. ISBN 0-9597594-0-9
First Published 1981
Japanese Edition 1983
Reprinted 1981, 1983, 1984, 1985, 1986, 1987
Overseas enquiries: NZ$9.95 mail to publisher
Also by Jan Bilton: Making the Most of Meat
New Zealand Microwave Cookbook
The Great New Zealand Cookbook
The New Zealand Dinner Party Cookbook
Summer Food
Fresh and Fancy Fare
Jan Biltons Tamarillo Cookbook
101 Creative Minced Meat Recipes

INTRODUCTION

The brown skinned, green fleshed kiwifruit grows on a vine in a similar manner to grapes. It ripens during the winter season — in N.Z., May to September. It is attractive, tasty and is high in Vitamin C, approximately 105mg/100g, more than the recommended daily requirement. It is low in kilojoules (calories) about 233kJ/100g, that is, 55.5 cals./3½ oz.

Storage : With the right conditions, kiwifruit will stay firm for 6 months. For this the temperature must be kept at 0°C (32°F) and the humidity should be 90-95%. Kiwifruit should not be stored with fruits or vegetables which emit ethylene gas as this accelerates the ripening process. At home, store the fruit in the refrigerator to maintain its firmness.

Ripening : Consumers — firm fruit could take from 1-4 weeks to become soft. To hasten ripening, place kiwifruit in a plastic bag with an apple or banana (both emit ethylene gas naturally) — hold at room temperature. The fruit will ripen in a few days. It is ready to eat when slightly soft to feel.

Coolstore fruit may be ripened similarly to bananas. When the fruit is at room temperature, it may be treated with the normal concentration of ethylene gas used to ripen bananas. The fruit should be held for 12-18 hours, then allowed to aerate naturally to remove all traces of the ripening gas. The fruit will soften within 2 days and will have a further shelf life of at least 7 days.

Eating : There is little waste in a kiwifruit. The whole fruit, even the skin, can be eaten — rub gently with a soft cloth to remove excess fur — use in savoury salads. Usually the fruit is peeled before eating or preparing in variety dishes. The simplest way of eating the fruit is to cut in half crosswise and scoop out the moist, refreshing flesh with a teaspoon.

Kiwifruit are known as 'kiwis' in many countries.

STARTERS

Create exotic starters to the day or dinner using kiwifruit.

Platter Foods

The emerald fruit may be used to its full advantage in its raw state, for it enhances the usual selection of canapés.

suggestions; (see photograph)
* crackers topped with pâté, sliced kiwifruit, beansprouts
* bread croûtons with kiwifruit and caviar
* rounds of bread, salami and kiwifruit
* quartered kiwifruit, sliced to form boats
* rye bread, creamed salmon and cream cheese, radish and kiwifruit
* vol au vents, smoked oysters and julienned kiwifruit

Open Sandwiches

suggestions;
* shredded lettuce, ham rolls, mayonnaise and kiwifruit slices
* pickled herrings, kiwifruit cubes, onion rings
* sliced pork, prunes and kiwifruit slices
* blue cheese, julienned kiwifruit, sieved egg yolk
* roast beef slices, pickled kiwifruit (recipe page 60), orange slices
* smoked eel, kiwifruit twist, black olives.

Use the little black seeds for decoration — they look like black caviar.

The Drink Section

Kiwifruit can be pureed and mixed with a variety of other juices to produce interesting combinations. To purée the fruit, mash well with a fork then sieve, or, purée in an electric blender or food processer. Take care not to over process and crush the seeds. These not only spoil the look of the puree but also make it slightly bitter. Process until just smooth then sieve to remove seeds.

The purée may be sweetened, ½ teaspoon sugar per kiwifruit, pulped and stored ready for use in the refrigerator, for up to 3 days. A dash of lemon juice maintains the colour.

Slices of kiwifruit can be used as decoration for drinks — on the side of the glass or inside the glass.

Brunch Beginner

1 banana
1 scoop vanilla ice cream
2 ice cubes
1 large kiwifruit, peeled
whipped cream
ground nutmeg

Blend banana, ice cream and ice until smooth. Pour into a glass. Blend kiwifruit until smooth. Spoon carefully on top of banana so colours do not mix. Top with a swirl of whipped cream and a sprinkling of nutmeg. Serves 1.

Kiwi Colada

1 cup ice cubes
½ cup coconut cream
½ cup kiwifruit purée
1 teaspoon caster sugar
½ cup white rum

Crush ice and place in 4 glasses. Combine remaining ingredients well and pour over ice. Serves 4.

Punch

6 cups orange juice
2 bottles sauterne
1 cup brandy
1 teaspoon bitters
ice
4 kiwifruit
1 bottle sparkling white wine, optional

Combine orange juice, sauterne, brandy and bitters. Pour over a large block of ice in a punch bowl. (Freeze some kiwifruit slices in the ice block). Add peeled and sliced kiwifruit and sparkling wine to the punch just before serving.

Cold Sour Kiwifruit Soup

There is a European influence to this summer soup. A good starter to a roast pork dinner. Do not over process the fruit — the crushed seeds will make the soup too bitter.

1 cup water
¼ cup sugar
2 cloves
1 tablespoon arrowroot
2 tablespoons cold water
500g (1 lb) kiwifruit
zest and juice of 1 large lemon
sour cream

In a medium saucepan, combine water and sugar until dissolved. Add cloves and bring to boil — boil 5 minutes then remove the cloves. Mix arrowroot to a paste with cold water, add to syrup and heat until thick. Reserve 1 kiwifruit for decoration. Peel remaining fruit and mash well or purée until just smooth. Sieve to remove seeds. Stir into cold syrup and chill for several hours. Before serving, stir in lemon zest and juice. Decorate the top with a little sour cream and diced kiwifruit. Serve ice cold. Serves 4.

Fried Camembert with Fruit

A saucy mixture of pineapple and kiwifruit is served with hot camembert. (Photograph page two)

2 camembert cheese
2 eggs, beaten
¾ cup dried breadcrumbs
oil for frying

Sauce : 300g (10 oz.) can of pineapple chunks (sweetened)
juice ½ lemon
dash Worcestershire sauce
1 tablespoon arrowroot
2 tablespoons water
2 kiwifruit, peeled and sliced

Cut each round of cheese into 4 wedges. Dip quarters in egg, then in breadcrumbs. Repeat this process.
Refrigerate to set coating. Meanwhile prepare sauce. Heat gently the pineapple, lemon juice and sauce. Thicken pineapple with arrowroot mixed to a smooth paste with water. Cook, stirring until thick.
To fry cheese, heat about 5mm (¼ in) oil in heavy pan over medium heat. Panfry cheese gently until golden on all sides — about 3 minutes. Add kiwifruit slices to sauce and warm through. Serve 2 pieces of cheese on 4 serving plates accompanied by the warm sauce. Serves 4.

Favourite Marinated Fish

This is always popular — fish marinated in cider vinegar and dressed up with a combination of ginger and green kiwifruit.

500g (1 lb) lean white fish, skinned and boned
1 small onion, diced
1 fresh or canned chilli, chopped
2.5cm (1 in) piece root ginger, grated
1 cup cider vinegar
3 kiwifruit
salt and pepper

Cut fish into bite-sized chunks. Place in bowl. Combine onion, chilli, ginger and vinegar and pour over fish. Marinate in refrigerator for about 4 hours or until fish has a cooked appearance. Stir occasionally. Peel kiwifruit and cut into 1.5cm (¾ in) dice. Drain fish and combine with fruit. Season with salt and pepper. Serves 6 as an entrée.

Bacon Kiwi Breakfast

Rub excess fur from fruit. Cut in half lengthwise. Roll small strips of bacon and secure with wooden cocktail sticks. Insert 2 sticks of bacon onto the cut face of the fruit. Grill under medium heat about 4 minutes. Serve immediately for breakfast or brunch.

Oriental Salad

Serve as a starter or as an accompaniment to a main course.

½ cup oil
1 tablespoon cider vinegar
1 tablespoon soy sauce
1 clove garlic, crushed
1 cm (½ in) piece root ginger, finely grated
1 medium onion
water
3 kiwifruit
1 cup bean shoots
½ cup sliced water chestnuts
3 small tomatoes, quartered

To make dressing, combine oil, vinegar, soy sauce, garlic and ginger — mix well or place in a blender or food processor. Slice onion finely — cook 5 minutes in boiling water. Drain and cool. Toss in dressing. Peel kiwifruit and slice lengthwise, then into 5mm (¼ in) strips. Just before serving, combine onion, fruit, bean shoots and chestnuts and spoon into 4 cocktail glasses. Top each glass with 3 tomato quarters. Serves 4.

Green Tomatoes

Halve medium sized tomatoes and scoop out flesh. Peel and finely dice kiwifruit and toss carefully with chopped fresh herbs. Season with salt and pepper. Spoon into tomato halves. Can be served as a main course vegetable or entrée with sardines.

Kiwifruit and Caviar

Large kiwifruit are halved, scooped out and refilled with caviar and prawns. A novel starter.

3 large kiwifruit
18 large prawns (but not king size)
3 tablespoons black or red caviar
salt and pepper

Cut kiwifruit in half using a zigzag movement. Carefully scoop out the flesh, leaving about 5mm (¼ in) around the outside edge. Cut flesh into 5mm (¼ in) dice. Select 6 cocktail sticks and thread 2 prawns onto each. Dice remaining prawns. Mix with diced kiwifruit, caviar and seasonings. Set kiwifruit shells firmly into 6 egg cups. Carefully fill with the combined ingredients. Top with skewered prawns. Serve on a plate surrounded by tiny squares of buttered rye bread. Serves 6.

Green Eggs and Ham

A variation on eggs mayonnaise.

4 hard boiled eggs
½ cup mild flavoured thick mayonnaise
1 large kiwifruit
1 cup very finely diced ham

Peel hard boiled eggs. Cut in half lengthwise and place side by side on 4 small serving plates. Peel kiwifruit and mash well. Combine with mayonnaise. Mixture should be of coating consistency. Carefully spoon over eggs to coat. Sprinkle diced ham around perimeter of eggs — on the serving plate. Serves 4 as an entrée.

male flower   *female flower*

For the vines to produce fruit, it is necessary to cultivate both male and female plants. Flowers pictured on back cover.

MAINS

Kiwifruit colour and flavour complement so many main course meals. Meat, fish and poultry all benefit from the association of the kiwi green. To maintain the colour with hot foods, it is preferable to add the fruit at the end of the cooking time, so that it just warms through, but is still colourful.

On cooking, the fruit loses some of its colour but its tangy flavour should not be overlooked with pork, curries or in casseroles. It can often be used in place of pineapple, apples or oranges in meat dishes.

Meat Tenderiser

Kiwifruit contains an enzyme, 'actinidin', which is an effective meat tenderiser. It is similar to the enzyme, 'papain', in papaya. This enzyme acts on protein foods.

Tough cuts of meat, fish or poultry may be tenderised by:
a) slicing the fruit and placing on top of the meat, or
b) puréeing the fruit — 'fork' the meat and paint with the purée. This is the most effective method of tenderising. Allow to stand for 30 minutes per 2.5cm (1 in) of thickness. Meat may be wiped and grilled, or, for casseroles, the kiwifruit marinade may be added to the ingredients. Do not tenderise the meat too long as it could become mushy. Heat inactivates the enzyme.

Poisson Michel

Flounder, sole or lean white fish fillets may be used to prepare this gorgeous combination of orange juice, liqueur, cashews and kiwifruit.

1kg (2 lb) fish fillets or
4 small flounder or sole
flour
salt and pepper
100g (3½ oz) butter
100g (3½ oz) cashew nuts
¼ cup orange flavoured liqueur
juice of 2 oranges
2-3 kiwifruit, peeled and sliced

Cut fillets into even sized pieces. Wipe dry. Dredge fish in lightly seasoned flour. In a large, heavy pan, melt half the butter over medium heat. Sauté fish quickly on each side until just golden. Place on a warm platter and into oven 150°C (300°F) while preparing sauce — about 5 minutes. Melt remaining butter in pan. Sauté cashews until golden. Pour in liqueur and flame. Lift out nuts with slotted spoon and place to one side. Add juice to pan and simmer until reduced and thick. Meanwhile top fish with kiwifruit slices and nuts and warm through in oven. Pour sauce over fish and serve immediately. Serves 4.

Fried Shrimp and Sour Sauce

A tangy sauce accompanies battered and crisp fried shrimp.
Serve with rice.

1 cup pineapple juice
1/2 cup vinegar
4 tablespoons tomato paste
4 tablespoons sugar
1/2 cup water
1/2 teaspoon salt
2 tablespoons cornflour (cornstarch)
3 kiwifruit
3/4 cup flour
salt and pepper
1 egg
3/4 cup iced water
1kg (2 lb) fresh shrimp or prawns
oil for frying

Combine juice, vinegar, tomato paste, sugar, water and salt
and bring to boil. Mix cornflour to a smooth paste with a
little cold water. Add to sauce and heat, stirring until thick.
Peel and slice kiwifruit. Whisk flour, seasonings, egg and
water to make a smooth batter. Peel shrimps and
pat dry. Dip in batter and deep fry 190°C (375°F) until
golden. Add kiwifruit to sauce and warm through. Pour
over shrimp and serve. Serves 6.

Scallop Salad Supreme

Poached scallops are combined with diced onion, red skinned apples, walnuts and kiwifruit. If scallops are unobtainable, try with cooked lobster or crayfish cubes.

10 fresh scallops
1 cup dry white wine
water
bouquet garni
1 large red apple
1 medium onion
1/2 cup walnut halves
2 large kiwifruit
1 tablespoon olive oil
freshly ground rock salt and black pepper
spinach leaves

Trim scallops. Place in saucepan with wine and sufficient water to just cover scallops. Add bouquet garni and slowly bring to boiling point — poach 5 minutes until tender. Drain and slice. Just before serving, combine diced apple, diced onion, walnuts and peeled and diced kiwifruit. Sprinkle over olive oil and season with salt and pepper. Serve on spinach leaves. Serves 4.

Traditional Lamb with Emerald Mint Sauce

Leg of lamb is roasted on medium heat for a short time and glazed with redcurrant jelly. The customary mint sauce is replaced by the bright emerald sauce which tastes so good with the lamb — New Zealands' national roast.

1 leg lamb, approx. 2kg (4 lb)
¼ cup redcurrant jelly

Place meat fat side up in roasting pan. Bake 180°C (350°F) for 20-25 minutes per 500g (1 lb). Brush regularly with warmed redcurrant jelly. Serve hot or cold. Serves about 8.

Sauce: 3-4 kiwifruit
　　　　1 teaspoon lemon juice
　　　　1 teaspoon sugar
　　　　3 tablespoons finely chopped fresh mint

Peel fruit and mash well or place in food processor or blender until just puréed. Stir in lemon juice, sugar and mint, and serve with hot or cold lamb. Makes 1 cup approximately.

Lamb Noisette Hayward

A loin of lamb is boned and rolled, baked and basted, sliced and served. The basting sauce is basically kiwifruit with oriental additions.

1 boned and rolled loin of lamb, about 1.5 kg (3lb)
1 large kiwifruit
2 teaspoons finely chopped root ginger
1 clove garlic, crushed
2 teaspoons soy sauce
1 tablespoon brown sugar
kiwifruit for garnish

Trim excess fat from lamb. Roll and tie with string every 4cm (1½ in). Peel kiwifruit, mash well and combine in saucepan with all other ingredients. Simmer 1 minute. Place meat in oven dish just large enough to hold it. Bake in oven 160°C (325°F) for 50-60 minutes basting often with the kiwifruit mixture. Place lamb on platter, cut into noisettes between each string. Remove strings. Turn cut face up. Serve hot or cold topped with slice of kiwifruit. One loin will make about 5-6 noisettes. Serve 1 per person.

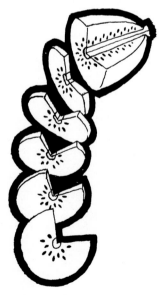

Herbed Veal Escalopes

Thinly sliced veal is wrapped around ham, kiwifruit and fresh herbs.

4 veal escalopes
2 slices ham
1 large kiwifruit
flour
1 tablespoon finely chopped fresh herbs (marjoram, thyme)
1 tablespoon oil
2 tablespoons butter
¼ cup white wine
finely chopped parsley

Flatten veal until 5mm (¼ in) thick. Cut slices of ham in half. Place on one half of each escalope (or schnitzel). Peel and slice kiwifruit into 4 rounds. Dip in flour and place on top of the ham. Sprinkle with fresh, chopped herbs. Fold other half of meat over to enclose filling to form a packet. Seal edges well. Dip in flour, shake off excess. Heat oil and butter in frypan. Add meat and cook over medium heat 2 minutes each side. Remove to warm platter. Add wine to pan, boil briskly until thick and spoon over meat. Sprinkle with parsley. Serves 4.

Japanese Style Pork

Thin slices of pork marinated and quickly fried, served with cabbage and kiwifruit makes a fast meal.

6 pork schnitzels
1 small clove garlic
1 teaspoon sugar
1 teaspoon finely grated root ginger
6 tablespoons Japanese soy sauce
6 tablespoons mirin or dry sherry
2 tablespoons oil
3 large kiwifruit
2 cups very finely shredded red cabbage
2.5cm (1 in) knob root ginger, grated (extra)

Place pork in a single layer on a flat plate. Crush garlic with sugar and mix with ginger, soy sauce and mirin (cooking sake). Pour over pork and leave for 30 minutes. Drain meat. Heat oil on heavy skillet and panfry meat quickly on high temperature, about 1 minute each side. Remaining marinade may be boiled and reduced and served spooned over the meat. Serve with peeled and sliced kiwifruit, and red cabbage, topped with grated root ginger. May be accompanied with boiled short grain rice. Serves 6.

Skewered Pork

Pork and kiwifruit are skewered and grilled.

500g (1lb) lean pork fillet (tenderloin)
2 tablespoons honey
2 tablespoons soy sauce
3 tablespoons oil
4 kiwifruit
1 tablespoon brown sugar

Cut pork into 2.5cm (1 in) cubes. Combine honey, soy sauce and 1 tablespoon oil. Mix well. Marinate meat in this mixture 1 hour. Peel kiwifruit and cut in half crosswise, or in quarters if very large. Mix remaining oil with brown sugar. Thread meat and kiwifruit alternately along 3 or 4 skewers. Brush fruit with oil mixture. Place under hot grill (or over barbecue) and cook, turning and basting occasionally about 8 minutes, until meat and fruit are lightly browned. Serves 3-4.

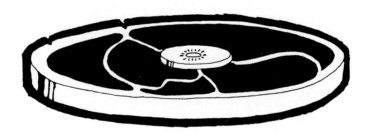

Ham Steaks

Panfry ham steaks both sides in butter, sprinkling with brown sugar after turning. Serve accompanied with panfried kiwifruit slices.

Indian Beef

Curry is seasoned with bacon, kiwifruit and spices and is topped with sugar coated kiwifruit slices.

800g (1¾ lb) blade or other stewing beef steak
2 tablespoons flour
salt and pepper
1 tablespoon curry powder
½ teaspoon mixed spice
2 slices bacon
2 tablespoons oil
1 tablespoon butter
2 tablespoons sugar
grated rind 1 lemon
¼ cup each water, sherry, lemon juice
2 kiwifruit, peeled and sliced in 1cm (½ in) rounds
caster sugar

Cut meat into 2.5cm (1 in) cubes. Combine flour and seasoning. Toss meat in mixture pressing well in. Panfry diced bacon in oil and butter until crisp. Add meat a little at a time and fry until golden on all sides. Add sugar, lemon rind, water, sherry, lemon juice and 1 sliced kiwifruit. Cover and simmer on low heat 2 hours until tender, adding more water if curry becomes too dry. Serve on a bed of rice topped with a ring of kiwifruit slices which have been dipped in caster sugar. Serves 6.

Curry Accompaniment

Finely diced kiwifruit served plainly or mixed with onion, ginger and mustard seeds, and combined with yoghurt, makes an ideal food to serve with a curry.

Southland Fried Chicken

Crispy chicken pieces served with fried kiwifruit and bananas.

2kg (4 lb) chicken joints
¼ cup lemon juice
½ cup white wine
2 tablespoons oil
salt and pepper
flour
2 eggs beaten
1½ cups dried breadcrumbs
60g (2 oz) ground almonds
oil
2 bananas
3 kiwifruit

Place chicken joints in a shallow dish. Combine lemon juice, wine, oil, salt and pepper. Pour over chicken and marinate 2 hours. Drain chicken and pat dry. Dip in flour, then beaten egg, then combined breadcrumbs and ground almonds. Press well in. Heat 1cm (½ in) oil in a large frypan and fry gently about 35 minutes on medium heat, turning when first side is golden. Meanwhile prepare fruit. Cut bananas in 3 lengths and kiwifruit into 1cm (½ in) slices. Dip in flour, egg and breadcrumbs. Panfry 1 minute each side in hot oil and serve with the chicken. Serves 6.

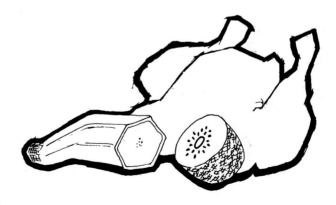

Chicken and Orange Blossom Sauce

Baked chicken pieces are smothered in an orange and kiwifruit sauce and garnished with orange blossom.

2kg (4 lb) chicken cut into joints
1/2 cup flour
1 teaspoon salt
125g (4 oz) butter, melted

Sauce : 1 cup orange juice
2 tablespoons lemon juice
1/3 cup brown sugar
1 tablespoon soy sauce
1 tablespoon cornflour (cornstarch)
3 kiwifruit, peeled and cut into 1cm (1/2 in) cubes
sesame seeds
orange blossoms (if available)

Shake chicken portions in plastic bag with flour and salt — coat well. Brush large baking pan with melted butter. Add chicken and brush with remaining butter. Bake 50 minutes at 180°C (350°F) turning chicken half-way during cooking. Meanwhile make the sauce. Combine juice, sugar, soy sauce and thickening. Bring to the boil and stir until thick. Add kiwifruit and warm through. Serve sauce spooned over cooked chicken pieces on a serving platter. Sprinkle with sesame seeds and garnish with orange blossoms. Serves 6.

Continental Sausage Casserole

Kiwifruit adds tang to this sausage and red cabbage dinner.

¼ of a medium red cabbage, shredded finely
2 tablespoons butter
1 onion, diced
3 tablespoons brown or raw sugar
4 large continental sausages e.g. Thuringer, Rookwurst
2 kiwifruit

Place cabbage in pan of boiling water — boil 1 minute and drain. Melt butter in pan and sauté onion until soft. Place cabbage and onion in greased casserole. Sprinkle with brown sugar. Cover and bake 180°C (350°F) for 30 minutes. Meanwhile stand sausages in hot water or prepare as per manufacturer's instructions. Peel kiwifruit and slice into 5mm (¼ in) rounds. Remove casserole from oven. Add sausages and kiwifruit. Cover again and bake a further ½ hour. Serves 4.

DESSERTS

The kiwifruit is well suited to glamorous endings. Simple but delicious desserts can be made by just slicing the fruit, sprinkling with sugar and a little of your favourite liqueur. Its uses are limited only by imagination.

'Actinidin', the meat tenderising enzyme in kiwifruit, also causes gelatine to break down. Therefore raw kiwifruit and gelatine cannot be combined in recipes. The fruit must be cooked first to inactivate the enzyme before being used in this type of dessert.

Agar-agar, a vegetable setting agent (from health and oriental stores) can be used as a substitute to set kiwifruit in jellies. Agar-agar looks like powdered gelatine — use 3/4 teaspoon to set 1 cup liquid.

On cooking, the kiwifruit developes quite a 'gooseberry' like flavour which is excellent for pies and puddings where flavour is of the utmost importance.

Pavlova

New Zealand's national dessert. A crisp shell of meringue with a marshmellow centre is topped with whipped cream and fruit.

2 egg whites
1½ cups caster sugar
½ teaspoon vanilla
1 teaspoon white vinegar
1 teaspoon cornflour (cornstarch)
4 tablespoons boiling water

Place all ingredients into a medium sized bowl and beat with a rotary or electric beater until mixture is smooth, shiny and stiff — about 12 minutes. Meanwhile place a sheet of greaseproof paper on a baking tray. Brush lightly with melted butter and dust with a little cornflour — shake off excess. Spoon meringue mixture onto prepared tray, forming a 23cm (9 in) circle. Bake in middle of oven, 180°C (350°F) for 10 minutes, reduce heat to 150°C (300°F) and bake a further 45 minutes. Allow to cool in oven.

Filling: 1¼ cups cream,
1 tablespoon icing (confectioner's) sugar
sliced kiwifruit, strawberries etc.,

Whip cream with icing sugar until stiff. Spread on top of cooled pavlova. Top with fruit. Serves about 6.

Glazed Fruit Flan

Can be made either in a pastry or biscuit crumb shell.

1 baked 20-23cm (8-9 in) flan shell
2 cups sour cream
1/3 cup icing (confectioner's) sugar
zest of 1/2 orange
2 teaspoons orange juice
1 teaspoon vanilla
2-3 kiwifruit
grapes
3 tablespoons sieved apricot jam

Beat cream and icing sugar until smooth — add zest, juice and vanilla. Spoon into prepared pie shell. Peel and slice kiwifruit and place with the grapes in an attractive pattern on top of the filling. Warm the apricot jam slightly and brush over the fruit. Serves 6-8.

Flan Pastry

2 cups flour
1 tablespoon sugar
1/4 teaspoon baking powder
pinch salt
100g (3 1/2 oz) butter
1 egg yolk
1 teaspoon lemon juice

Sift dry ingredients, rub in butter until mixture resembles coarse breadcrumbs. Mix to a firm dough with egg yolk and lemon juice. Add a little iced water a tablespoon at a time, if too dry. Knead lightly, wrap and refrigerate 30 minutes. Roll out to fit a 20-23cm (8-9 in) flan tin. Line base and sides gently, trim off excess. Prick base with fork. Bake 10-15 minutes 180°C (350°F) until golden. Cool in tin.

Individual Tarts

Fresh kiwifruit is topped with meringue or glazed with jam.

1 quantity flan pastry
4-5 kiwifruit
6 teaspoons sugar

Prepare pastry and chill. Divide into 6 equal portions. Roll out each piece to fit base and sides of 6, 10cm (4 in) flan tins. Bake 10 minutes at 180°C (350°F). Cool. Peel and slice kiwifruit into flans. Sprinkle each with a teaspoon of sugar. Use toppings suggested below. Serves 6.

Kiwifruit Meringue Pies

Beat 2 egg whites until frothy, add ¼ cup caster sugar and contine beating until stiff and shiny. Spoon over fruit. Bake 200°C (400°F) for about 4 minutes until meringue is golden.

French Tarts

Brush kiwifruit filled tarts with ⅓ cup redcurrant jelly which has been warmed with 1 tablespoon kirsch. Refrigerate 1 hour. Dust with icing (confectioner's) sugar before serving.

Biscuit Shell

225g (8 oz) plain or chocolate flavoured biscuits
125g (4 oz) butter, melted

Crush biscuits finely, pour in melted butter. Press evenly over sides and base of a 20-23cm (8-9 in) greased flan tin. Bake 180ºC (350ºF) for 12 minutes. Cool.

Hazelnut Meringue Cake

Layers of hazelnut meringue are sandwiched with liqueur flavoured cream and kiwifruit — see cover.

75g (3 oz) hazelnuts
3 egg whites
3/4 cup caster sugar
4-5 kiwifruit
300ml (1/2 pint) cream
1 tablespoon icing (confectioner's) sugar
1 tablespoon orange flavoured liqueur

Toast hazelnuts under a hot grill 3-4 minutes. Rub with a clean cloth to remove skins — discard. Place nuts in a blender or food processor and chop very finely. Beat egg whites until stiff, add half the sugar and beat until smooth. Carefully fold in remaining sugar and hazelnuts. Cover baking tray with non-stick baking paper (or prepare as for pavlova tray) and make 3 even circles of meringue mixture, about 18cm (7 in) in diameter. (One circle may have to be cooked on another tray). Bake in cool oven 150°C (300°F) for 1 hour reducing temperature to 110°C (225°F) for 2 hours — cook until dry and crisp. Layers may be stored in an airtight container until required. To prepare filling, peel kiwifruit, halve lengthwise and slice across. Whip cream and sugar until stiff, fold in liqueur. Spread 1/4 of the cream on top of the one layer of meringue cake — add a few slices of kiwifruit. Top with another layer of meringue, spread with more cream and fruit. Place top layer of cake on, spread with remaining cream and decorate with kiwifruit slices. Serves 8.

Phylo Triangles

Slices of kiwifruit are wrapped in paper-thin Greek phylo pastry purchased at the delicatessen. They are deep fried until crisp and served hot.

4 sheets phylo pastry
3-4 kiwifruit, peeled
safflower oil
caster sugar

Use 1 sheet of pastry at a time. Cut each sheet into 8cm (3 in) wide strips. Brush each strip with a little oil. Slice kiwifruit into 5mm (¼ in) rounds. Place one kiwifruit slice on the end of each pastry strip. Take corner of pastry and fold over to form a triangle, covering the kiwifruit. Lift first triangle up and over to form second triangle. Continue folding over and over until the end of the pastry strip is reached. When all pastry triangles have been prepared, lower, a few at a time into deep, hot oil. Fry until golden — drain well. Serve sprinkled with caster sugar. Makes 16 triangles enough to serve 4-6 people.

Pancakes Regal

Filled with a tasty mixture of fruit, apricot jam and nuts.

Pancakes: 6 tablespoons flour
1/4 teaspoon salt
2 teaspoons sugar
2 eggs
3/4 cup milk
1 tablespoon oil
butter or oil for frying

Sift dry ingredients into a bowl. Beat eggs, add to dry ingredients. Mix in milk and oil. Stand 2 hours. Heat a small heavy pancake pan, swirl a little butter or oil over the surface. Spoon 2-3 tablespoons batter into the pan — swirl mixture to cover pan. Cook until golden, about 1 minute each side. Repeat until all mixture is used, stacking crêpes as they are cooled. Makes about 12.

Filling: 1/2 cup sieved apricot jam
zest and juice of 1 lemon
1/4 cup chopped toasted almonds
1 banana, diced
2-3 kiwifruit, peeled and diced
icing (confectioner's) sugar

Heat jam, zest, lemon juice and nuts — pour over fruit and gently heat through — do not allow fruit to change colour. Spoon a little of the mixture into each crêpe and fold over. Place 2 on each serving plate and dust with icing sugar. Serve with whipped or sour cream. Serves 6.

Moulded Jellies

Agar-agar is the setting substance used to gel cubes of kiwifruit in mandarin syrup. A good dessert for after an oriental style meal.

300g (11 oz) can mandarin segments
water
1¼ teaspoons powdered agar-agar
4 large kiwifruit
4 tablespoons chopped crystallised ginger

Drain mandarins retaining their juice. Place mandarins to one side. Strain juice and make up to 1½ cups with water. Sprinkle over the agar-agar and simmer about 5 minutes, until dissolved. Cool. Peel kiwifruit and dice. Place in 4 individual moulds with ginger. Pour cold jelly mixture over fruit to just cover. Refrigerate. Agar-agar sets very quickly. When quite solid, jellies may be inverted onto serving plates. Decorate tops with mandarin segments in spoke-like formation. Serves 4.

Kiwifruit Ice Cream

Always best if freshly made.

6 large kiwifruit
150g (5 oz) caster sugar
3 eggs separated
1¼ cups cream, whipped

Peel and mash fruit — leave some pieces lumpy. Stir in half the sugar and stand for 15 minutes. Separate eggs. Beat yolks and remaining sugar over hot water until thick and creamy — cool. Beat whites until stiff. Fold both into the fruit with whipped cream. Freeze quickly. Place in suitable container into the coldest part of the freezer. Freeze until mushy, stir then freeze until solid. Serves about 6.

Kiwifruit Sorbet

This is delicious — kiwifruit purée sweetened with sugar syrup and frozen. It is slightly softer than ice cream and should be served in chilled glasses. Often called sherbets, granita or water ices.

¾ cup sugar
2 cups water
zest and juice of 1 lemon
6 large kiwifruit

Dissolve sugar in water, add zest and juice — boil steadily for 10 minutes. Chill. Peel, mash and sieve kiwifruit. There should be about 2 cups pulp. Combine pulp with equal amounts of cold sugar syrup. Place in freezer in suitable container — freeze until mushy. Beat well and freeze until stiff. Serves 6-8.

Special Treat

On special occasions the Kiwifruit Sorbet could be served in hollowed kiwifruit shells or in hollow red apples. Cut across top of apples and remove these 'hats'. Scoop out inside of apple — this can be cooked for later use. Fill inside of apple with the sorbet and serve topped with the red apple 'hats'.

Sauce

Pulp kiwifruit by mashing well with a fork or placing in a blender or food processor for a short time. Sieve. Remember not to over process the fruit — the crushed seeds give a speckly appearance to the sauce and cause it to taste bitter. Add 1 teaspoon caster sugar, icing sugar or sugar syrup to each kiwifruit pulped. A dash of lemon juice and/or liqueur may be added to taste.

This makes a delicious ice cream topping or topping for cheesecakes or raw fruit. It may be prepared in bulk and frozen.

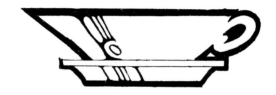

Kiwiana Yoghurt

2 bananas
1 cup plain yoghurt
2 tablespoons cream
1 tablespoon sugar
½ cup kiwifruit sauce
2 egg whites

Mash bananas coarsely and combine with yoghurt cream and sugar. Fold in kiwifruit sauce. Whip egg whites until stiff and fold into the yoghurt mixture. Spoon into serving dishes. Serves 4.

Walnut Gâteau

Layers of walnut cake are sandwiched with jam and smothered in cream cheese, nuts and kiwifruit.

4 eggs
3/4 cup caster sugar
1 1/4 cups self raising flour
1/4 cup finely chopped walnuts
3 tablespoons hot water
1 teaspoon butter
kiwifruit or apricot jam
250g cream cheese
2 tablespoons icing (confectioner's) sugar
1/2 teaspoon vanilla essence
3/4 cup coarsely chopped walnuts
1 large kiwifruit, peeled and sliced

Beat eggs until light and fluffy. Gradually beat in sugar until mixture is thick and sugar completely dissolved. Sift flour over egg mixture and fold in with finely chopped walnuts. Quickly fold in hot water in which butter has been melted. Pour into a deep, greased, 20cm (8 in) round cake tin. Bake at 180°C (350°F) approximately 25 minutes. Turn onto a cake cooler to cool. Slice cake horizontally into 3 layers and sandwich together again with either kiwifruit jam (recipe page 59) or apricot jam. Beat cream cheese with sugar and essence until light. Cover top and sides of cake with cream cheese. Press coarsley chopped walnuts on sides. Ridge top in circular lines with a fork. Before serving place kiwifruit slices around the top.

Kiwi Madeira

Sliced kiwifruit are cooked in the cake which is reminiscent of apple cake.

200g (7 oz) butter
1 cup sugar
3 eggs
1 cup self raising flour
½ cup cornflour (cornstarch)
2 thinly sliced kiwifruit

Cream butter and sugar until light. Add eggs one at a time, beating well after each addition. Sift flour and cornflour. Mix well. Add kiwifruit. Lightly grease and line base of a 20cm (8 in) square cake tin. Pour in cake mixture. Bake 180°C (350°F) for 50 minutes. Turn off oven and leave cake in oven a further 20 minutes. May be served warm with morning coffee, but keeps well in cool place. Top may be iced or sprinkled with a little caster sugar.

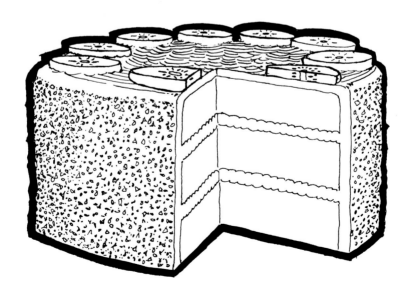

Special Brandy Snaps

These brandy snaps are left flat, not rolled, and sandwiched with cream and kiwifruit.

2 tablespoons golden syrup
60g (2½ oz) butter
⅓ cup brown sugar
½ cup flour
2 teaspoons ground ginger
pinch salt

Filling: 1½ cups cream
        1 tablespoon icing (confectioner's) sugar
        1 tablespoon Galliano or other liqueur
        3 kiwifruit

Place syrup, butter and sugar into a saucepan. Stir over low heat until butter is melted. Sift flour, ginger and salt into a bowl. Stir in butter mixture. Drop small teaspoonfuls of mixture onto greased trays, allowing room for spreading. Bake 180°C (350°F) for about 5 minutes until golden. Remove from oven, allow to cool on trays 1 minute before placing on a wire cake rack to cool. Whip cream with sugar and liqueur. Peel kiwifruit, cut in half lengthwise and slice. Sandwich 2 brandy snaps together with cream and kiwifruit. Pipe a rosette of cream on top and garnish with a kiwifruit slice.

Baked Kiwifruit with Nut Topping

Tangy hot kiwifruit have a topping of almonds and walnuts.

4 large kiwifruit
2 tablespoons brown sugar
2 tablespoons apricot jam or orange marmalade
50g (2 oz) butter
¾ cup flour
2 tablespoons sugar
¾ cup chopped mixed blanched almonds and walnuts
2 tablespoons sherry
whipped cream
nutmeg

Peel and slice kiwifruit into a baking dish. Sprinkle with brown sugar and spread with jam. Rub butter into flour with fingertips — add sugar and nuts. Spread over the fruit. Bake 190°C (375°F) for 20 minutes. Sprinkle with sherry and serve hot with whipped cream with a dash of nutmeg added. Serves 4-5.

Soufflé in Chocolate Case

Takes time to prepare but will win compliments.

Chocolate case; 200g block plain dark chocolate

Break chocolate into pieces. Place in a strong plastic bag and hold in hot water until just melted. Snip a corner off the bag and squeeze chocolate out into a small warm bowl. Line a 19cm (7 in) deep round cake tin with baking paper or foil allowing a 5cm (2 in) collar above the lip of the tin. With a pastry brush, carefully paint chocolate on base and sides of lined cake tin about 5cm (2 in) high. Chocolate should be even around the top and thick enough to hold the soufflé mixture. Refrigerate until set.

Soufflé; 4 large kiwifruit
       zest and juice of 1 orange and 1 lemon
       4 eggs, separated
       ½ cup sugar
       3 teaspoons powdered gelatine
       ¼ cup water
       1 cup cream, whipped
       chopped nuts
       diced kiwifruit

Mash kiwifruit and sieve. Place in top part of double boiler with zest, fruit juices, egg yolks and sugar. Stir briskly over hot water until mixture thickens. Remove from heat and cool. Soak gelatine in cold water 10 minutes then dissolve over low heat. Add to fruit mixture and leave until just beginning to set. Whip egg whites until stiff. Whip cream. Carefully fold egg whites into fruit mixture, then the cream. Pour into soufflé dish — the mixture should rise about 4cm (1½ in) above top of chocolate soufflé case. Refrigerate until set. To serve, remove soufflé by lifting out by the paper collar. Peel off paper. Decorate side with chopped nuts and top with diced kiwifruit. Serves 8.

Cream Fondue

For this, a spirit burner is required, an earthenware fondue pot and fondue forks.

2 cups cream
1 cup icing (confectioner's) sugar
2 tablespoons cornflour (cornstarch)
1 tablespoon kirsch or other liqueur
4-6 kiwifruit
sponge cake

Mix 1¾ cups cream and icing sugar in fondue pot. Heat gently, stirring until melted. Combine remaining cream with cornflour and stir into fondue pot until thick. Add liqueur. Peel and quarter kiwifruit. Cut cake into 2.5cm (1 in) cubes. Place in bowls. With a fondue fork, each guest spears a piece of fruit or cake and dips it into the fondue sauce. If desired, the fondue sauce maybe poured into small, hot, ramekins and placed on plates with kiwifruit and cake. Guests then have their own individual dips. Serves 4-6.

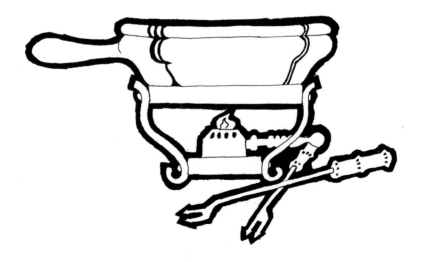

Steeped in Red Wine Kiwifruit

Serve very cold — best prepared 1 day in advance.

1½ cups good red wine
½ cup water
4 tablespoons sugar
6 kiwifruit
¼ teaspoon vanilla

Place wine in a saucepan and bring to boil; reduce by
boiling to half volume. Add water and sugar, cool and chill.
Peel kiwifruit and slice in half lengthwise. Stir vanilla into
red wine syrup, add kiwifruit and chill. Serves 4-6.

Caramelised

¾ cup sugar
1 cup water
4 kiwifruit
4 tablespoons chopped preserved ginger in syrup, or
orange zest

Dissolve sugar in water then boil until just golden —
about 10 minutes. Peel and slice kiwifruit into 4 serving
dishes. Spoon the cool caramel over the fruit.
Refrigerate until chilled. Serve topped with chopped
ginger, or orange zest. May be accompanied with
yoghurt or cream. Serves 4.

Fruit Salad

Kiwifruit combine well with everyday and exotic fruits to provide memorable salads.

Juice of 2 oranges
1 tablespoon of your favourite liqueur
1 tablespoon raw sugar
454g (1 lb) can lychees, drained
1 small papaya
4-5 kiwifruit

Combine orange juice, liqueur and sugar — stir until dissolved. Place lychees in salad bowl. Peel, deseed and cube the papaya and add with peeled and sliced kiwifruit to bowl. Pour over the orange juice. Nuts (almonds, brazils, or hazelnuts) make good additions. Serves 8.

Other combinations:

kiwifruit with sliced oranges and ginger
strawberries and walnuts
banana and long thread coconut
canned mandarins and marshmellows

Flambéd!

Simple — the microwave oven is ideal for cooking these also (cook ½ minute per skewer).

6 kiwifruit
2 tablespoons brown or white sugar
¼ cup brandy, warmed
desiccated coconut, optional

Peel kiwifruit. Cut into quarters. Thread onto 4 skewers. Place in an attractive, shallow, baking dish — sprinkle with sugar. Place in oven 190°C (375°F) for about 5 minutes, until just warm but still colourful. Take dish to table, pour over warmed brandy and ignite. Swish juice around dish. Sprinkle with coconut and serve with cream or ice cream. Serves 4.

MISCELLANEOUS

Freezing

Choose firm but mature fruit. Peel and slice thickly, about 7mm (5/8 in) minimum. Add 1 tablespoon lemon juice per cup of fruit to retain colour.

a) May be placed in a single layer on a tray and frozen the free-flow method. Once frozen, slices can be stored in airtight bag or container. To use, remove from freezer 5 minutes before required, or thaw in refrigerator 15 minutes. Use immediately in salads or on cakes.

b) Place slices in medium syrup (2 cups water, 1 cup sugar). Freeze. To use, thaw and use as is in desserts.

c) Slices may be frozen with sugar — 1 part sugar to 4 parts fruit. To use, thaw and use as a dessert with cream or use in hot pies and puddings.

d) Pulp — To each cup of pulp add 1 tablespoon lemon juice and 1 tablespoon sugar. Fruit may be sieved to remove seeds. To use, add to drinks, as a topping for flans, cakes or ice cream.

e) Whole — do not peel but rub off excess fur. Place in plastic bag and seal and freeze. To use, peel and cook from frozen state in savoury casseroles or cooked desserts.

Drying

The bright green colour of kiwifruit disappears during the drying process but the resulting product is good to chew. Sun can be used for drying but just the oven method is given here.

Use perfect, just ripe fruit. Peel kiwifruit and cut in half crosswise. Brush with lemon juice. In a single layer, spread on a rack covered in muslin. Place rack on a tray or in a roasting dish. Place in centre of oven leaving the door ajar. Turn heat to 50°C (120°F). Heat for 2 hours. Next day repeat the process — this should be repeated twice. (Use the oven heat after other cooking is finished). Fruit should be dried by this time. Stand in a cool dark place before storing in an airtight container. To use, fruit may be eaten as is, **or,** reconstituted by soaking in water for 2 hours, cooked with sugar and use as a filling for pies and puddings.

Fresh Fruit Jam

500g (1 lb) peeled, ripe or frozen kiwifruit
2½ cups caster sugar
1 tablespoon lemon juice
5 tablespoons liquid pectin

Purée fruit and place in bowl with sugar and juice. Stir to dissolve sugar. Cover and stand 20 minutes. Add pectin and stir 2 minutes. Spoon into small clean jars or plastic containers. Cover and stand 24 hours to set. Seal with wax. Store in refrigerator up to 5 weeks or freezer for 1 year. Makes a soft jam.

Kiwifruit Jam

1kg (2 lb) kiwifruit
juice 1 large lemon
⅓ cup water
4 cups sugar

Peel kiwifruit and slice into 5mm (¼ in) rounds. Place in a saucepan with lemon juice and water. Tie lemon peel and pips in muslin and add to pan. Bring to boil very slowly, stirring occasionally. Try to retain the shape of the fruit. Simmer until fruit is soft. Add sugar, stir until dissolved. Boil briskly until setting point is reached, [104°C (220°F)]. Remove muslin bag. Skim off any excess seeds floating on top. 2-3 drops of green food colouring may be added if desired. Pour into hot, clean jars and cover.

Brandied Kiwifruit

Peel kiwifruit and cut in half. Place in a clean dry jar. Sprinkle on an equal amount of sugar to fruit. Pour in enough brandy to cover the fruit. Seal jars preferably with plastic-coated metal lids. Store in a cool dark place for at least 4 months before using. Ideal for serving with coffee after dinner.

Bottled in Sauterne or Red Wine

2 cups sauterne or good red wine
½-1 cup sugar
1kg (2 lb) kiwifruit

If using sauterne add ½ cup sugar, to the red add 1 cup sugar. Heat wine and sugar, stirring until dissolved. Simmer 5 minutes. Peel fruit and cut in half lengthwise. Place in hot clean jars and cover with hot syrup to within 1.5cm (½ in) of the top.
either: seal and process in waterbath 20 minutes,
or: cover jars, place in centre of oven on a wad of newspaper. Heat 150°C (300°F) for 30 minutes. Remove jars and seal. Make excellent gifts.

Pickled

1kg (2 lb) kiwifruit
1 teaspoon whole cloves
1 teaspoon whole allspice
2.5cm (1 in) piece cinnamon stick
350g (12 oz) brown sugar
1 cup cider vinegar

Peel kiwifruit and cut in half lengthwise. Tie spices in muslin and heat with sugar and vinegar for 5 minutes. Place fruit in mixture and simmer gently 10 minutes. Carefully pack kiwifruit into clean jars. Pour over the hot liquid and seal while hot. Good with cold meats and cheeses.

INDEX

About the Author

Jan Bilton lives in Auckland, New Zealand. Since 1970 she has worked as a food consultant, a job that allowed her to work from home while her children were small. Initially most of Jan's work involved writing articles and giving lessons or demonstrations. As the business grew, so did the variety of work; product development and testing, recipe development, photography, product promotions and export.

Today Jan has the opportunity to work in interesting projects over a wide range of food related activities both in N.Z. and overseas. She finds the tremendous variety stimulating and challenging.

In this book, Jan uses all her training and experience. Her formal education at Otago University (Dip. H.Sc.), her recipe development and her knowledge of food for photography are obvious by reading this book. The New Zealand Kiwifruit Cookbook is as attractive as it is practical, a direct reflection of the author.

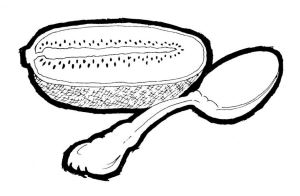